ASSEMBLY REQUIRED

A GUIDE TO BUILDING A POSITIVE MINDSET

TYRAE TOWNZEL SR.

TNT Publishing, LLC

CONTENTS

FOREWORD

DR. JASON JACKSON

Since the dawn of the Industrial Age, there have been concerns around repetitive work and human health. Now, in the Information Age, these concerns continue to persist and change, with influences such as pandemics, workplace automation, and civil distress bringing with them growing concerns of safety and security.

This book is useful to new employees and seasoned practitioners looking to be more positive at work and life.

My former student, mentee, and friend, Tyrae Townzel, Sr., brings his talents and gifts to this book to help you and others. His tacit knowledge of supply chain, quality, and positivity combine to a narrative with wisdom that will help you make the most of your individual day and collective team accomplishments!

There is no greater reward in life than helping

others fulfill their talents, dreams, and goals and then seeing them continue to help others with opportunities and a spirit of excellence. Together we will help society heal and grow into the positive place we want it to be. Tyrae is continuing the journey; I hope you will be inspired by it and take your next steps on the path too.

INTRODUCTION

Hello positive people, this book is dedicated to the trendsetters, go-getters, dream chasers, motivated and unmotivated, inspired and uninspired; it covers the gamut of people worldwide. There is more than enough negativity to go around in this world of Covid-19, social distancing, unemployment, quarantines, and civil unrest. Assembly Required is a guide created to show you how to build a positive mindset. As a professional assembler, student of life, and believer in total positivity, I would like to share my knowledge and techniques to create a positive mindset daily. Take the time to absorb the conveyed messages and see how they apply to you as an individual, some humorous, all real-life, examples that can go into your daily life and routine.

The two most important days in your life are your birth date and your death date. Everything in between is what builds your legacy as a human being, daughter, son, mother, father, and every other title you may receive along the way. Being positive is a choice and can be a way of life when you implement that mindset daily. Sure, you are right; every day may not be glorious, but we all have it inside ourselves to be the best person we can be each day. Positive people, these are facts to know and tell—both negativity and misery love company. Do not allow either into your life, realm, home, or work environment. The world is a much better place when we all work together to create harmony and brotherhood in the uncertain world we live in currently. I promise you that I will be doing my part to be part of the solution and not the problem.

Earning my bachelor's degree from Purdue University Global was a significant event in my life. At fifty-four years of age, the highest level was where I set the bar— creating my concept of having a positive mindset while working full-time, having shoulder surgery, and being away from work for seven months during the most challenging classes.

Positive people, believe me when I tell you; I was not only discouraged; I was questioning myself as to what I was doing. My life changed when I met Dr. Jason Jackson, one of my many professors at Purdue University Global, where I attended. Dr. Jackson challenged me to find the greatness inside myself; he had told me that he saw it firsthand, and now it was my mission to see it in myself. Indeed, the respect and admiration I had for Dr. Jackson was unwavering; he always told it like it was, telling you what you needed to hear and not what you wanted to hear.

It is a rare occurrence that you cross paths with someone in your life who is not immediate family, showing a genuine interest in the goals and dreams you are attempting to go after. Dr. Jackson did that for me, and on that day, I vowed to pay it forward and help others, everyone!

The three-year journey helped me realize that I could accomplish anything that I put my mind to, including writing this book to inspire people never to give up on their goals and aspirations. By the way, I graduated with honors, Magna Cum Laude, not too bad for an old dog.

The end goal is to bring positivity into people's lives and help others to find their better selves. We all have greatness inside of us; sometimes, we need help finding it. Building a positive mindset is the first step in the right direction, so with great distinction, I hope this guide helps you grow.

Special thanks to my number one fan, my mother, Sandra Bullock. The selflessness that I have comes from her heart, and I love you, mom.

THE LIFE OF A PRO ASSEMBLER

Positive people, this is where the journey begins; I have worked for a major manufacturer for over thirteen years. I have experienced several jobs in my tenure, and for the past three years, my position has been that of a professional assembler (pro assembler, moving forward).

The first thing that comes to my mind when I think of my job, pro assembler, is two words: redundant existence; imagine doing the same thing over and over. Day after day, month after month, year after year, you get the picture. Redundancy not only applies to assembly work; anyone can experience the same humdrummery in their personal life, position, or career.

The issue with assembly work is that you know what you will be facing each day. Some days are heavier than others, based on the type of machines we are building, and there are times when you know that you will be busting your butt for the entire day. On those days, I tell myself that it is going to be a paid workout day. Why not? There has never been a more valid statement made, I am getting paid, and I already know that I will be getting a workout. I instantaneously turn my day into a positive and prepare for the day ahead and all that comes with it.

Please do not get me wrong. First of all, I love my job and the beauty of being a pro assembler in a redundant existence. It allows you the opportunity for self-reflection, self-motivation, challenging yourself, and self-growth. Positivity drives me daily to be the best pro assembler possible and spread that positivity throughout the team.

You may not be able to change everyone, but if I can change a single person, I am on the right track to making the working environment better for everyone. Being a loyal teammate and valued employee, the daily goal that I set for myself is to change the work environment's culture—leading by example, closing or eliminating the gap between union and salary personnel, working together to build the highest quality machine possible. The customer's name on the windshield deserves it.

A positive mindset creates better communication, mutual respect, transparency, and builds trust with one another. These are the keys to having a successful and productive work experience. Your mindset and the vibe that you exude creates friendships and camaraderie with the other pro assemblers and the operations staff. Keep in mind; you spend more time with your teammates than you do with your family on certain occasions and during the build season duration.

Working amongst a diverse group of individuals, who are all pro assemblers, executing their job at the highest level, the expectation is to build a machine in a set time. The required time to make a machine is twenty-one minutes. When all cylinders are running at one hundred percent, the goal of twenty-one minutes or less cycle time will be achieved or exceeded. Positive and negative influences play a crucial factor in the success or failure of achieving the goal and the set number of machines that we build per shift, which we can say is twenty-one, just for a tangible visual for you.

On an assembly line with ninety people, all of different backgrounds, upbringing, races, nationalities, religions, preferences, and mindsets, there will always be room for disagreements, a difference of opinions, and sometimes just a disliking between two or more people. Let us keep it strictly one hundred percent, positive people.

We work in an environment inside of a different world. When dealing with many different personalities, the key is to share the knowledge with everyone involved that we have a common goal that we want to accomplish. The purpose is three-fold; to make a living, build the best machines possible, and be safe; going home the same way you came.

The reality of it, positive people, and we all know a few, we may fall into the same category ourselves, are the teammates or coworkers that come to work angry every day for no apparent reason. The ones that spend the day complaining about everything or those who love to gossip or instigate, fueling the fire between others in the work environment. Wasted energy is the name I have for that type of outlook, and the benefit of it is naught, nada, zero, and it serves no purpose!

It can be comical at times, but when that attitude or negativity hinders performance and productivity, it becomes a serious matter that needs to be corrected as soon as possible. Come on, y'all, are you with me?

I consider myself a leader, at work, at home, and in my community. As a leader, I intend to find common ground that everyone understands, which helps anyone who needs guidance, support, or encouragement. When you are a part of a team, you are part of a family, regardless of blood or not. Developing and growing with each other is what makes us better as people and as human beings. I have witnessed great things accomplished by working together and communicating with one another as a collective unit versus the division and negativity route.

Take into account, positive people, trust and believe that it is a fact that we have no control over ninety-nine percent of what goes on in the world around us, yet that one percent that we can control is being positive, not allowing negativity into your life, your realm, or your home. The first step is to realize that a positive mindset is attainable at any level of your life; one must take the initiative to start looking at life from a positive perspective.

A positive mindset enhances your experience, those around you can visually see the change in your spirit and the aura that glows from you like a beam of light. The blessings that we all possess as pro assemblers, gainful employment, excellent health insurance, family and friends, and the knowledge that the machines we build provide a livelihood for the person buying that machine, made with the highest quality.

The perspective that I am speaking of here is from my world as a pro assembler. Not being disillusioned with what is happening worldwide also provides the incentive to bring positivity into people's lives.

We are all affected by world events, and we can all build positive relationships with one another. All we need is everyone's effort; when I first started working at the company, I was a press operator. I had no experience operating a press machine, but I can tell you this. If you are not on point and paying attention, you can get seriously injured or even killed.

There were only two operators on the press machines in my area, Bob and myself. Bob had over thirty years when I started, and he was a character, 6'5" with a barbell mustache, and yes, Bob was white and straight old school. I never missed work, and for the first week, Bob did not say a single word to me. Not a greeting, a wave, nor any acknowledgment that I even existed.

I was over forty when I started, and I can take a hint when people don't talk to you or acknowledge you, so I went on about my business and did my job, keeping to myself. Now, this press job consisted of making parts, and in the process, you would create slugs that build up underneath the press machine. After several pieces were complete, you needed to clear out the built-up slugs. Otherwise, they would become jammed, and eventually, the pressure would cause a blowout. A blowout is when slugs shoot out from the machine and, depending on the slug size, the result would be the severe injury or fatality that I spoke of earlier.

It was my third week, and I cannot tell you why, but I forgot to clear the slugs. Bob was listening to my press strokes, and he walked down to me and asked, "When was the last time you cleared your slugs?" I said, "It has been a while; let me clear them right now." Thank the Lord that Bob came over when he did; I had so many slugs jammed in the machine that with a few more strokes I would have gotten hurt, with no one to blame but myself.

After that incident, Bob and I became the best of friends, and he started to share his knowledge with me. He had two favorite sayings; the first was, "I'm only going to show you this once," but he would show me multiple times if I needed help. His second was that I was a "stand-up guy," and that he did not know why he liked me, but he did, and then Bob would start laughing.

Bob and I would have drinks together after work, and he would tell me about the hellion he was growing up, and did he have some stories to tell. Bob retired a few years after I got there, but we always kept in touch; unfortunately, Bob passed away, and I lost one of the best friends I've ever had. Out of respect and homage, Bob's wife asked me to walk their daughter down the aisle for her wedding day. We may have looked like the odd couple, but that is what building a relationship is about, taking the time to get to know a person. People have more in common than you think, and as big as the world is, it is just as small. Being positive allows you to create friendships and relationships that can last a lifetime.

There are eight critical elements to success as a pro assembler; these elements have helped me build a positive mindset. As I see them, these are my creations, the things that I do, so here are the eight parts: focus, sequence, competition, challenges, quality-driven, the importance of efficiency, time management, and setting yourself up for success.

Every day in the assembly world brings new trials and tribulations; positive people can apply positive mindset elements in all life situations and any other job or career environment, not just assembly work. We will examine each component and define its importance and utilize it to build a positive mindset. Thank you for going on this journey with me. Come on, y'all!

BEING FOCUSED

I n assembly work, being focused is an essential element. Keeping your mind on the task at hand means the difference between working at the highest level and making mistakes and missing operations. As we know right now, life brings many aspects to it, easily distracting an individual. Personal issues, family issues, money issues, and the way of the world as we are all currently living provides an opportunity for distractions.

In a positive mindset, you learn to leave your issues at the gate, you have a job to do, and the assembly team is counting on you to come in and be at your best. You are individually responsible for your respective station; you are an integral part of a collective group of pro assemblers that work in unison to build the best machines possible at the highest quality level.

My positive mindset distinguishes different types of focus, these are self-interpreted meanings, but as you read the definitions, maybe you can visualize my intention. There are three types of focus: Focus, Laser focus, and Total focus.

Focused: Being focused is when you pay attention to the job at hand, or in a life situation, you take the necessary steps to complete a task or to achieve a goal. When you are focused, you may be working at a high level, yet on occasion, you can get sidetracked and lose sight of the task at hand and make mistakes or forget steps in your operation. A positive mindset emphasizes focusing on the task at hand and being aware.

Have you ever been working on something at home, maybe a DIY project, and you promise yourself that you are going to get it done today? You are cruising along, making headway finishing your project, then the phone rings or a friend stops by with a twelve-pack. You are on the phone with your brother, and you get to talking about going fishing, or you tell your friend that you can drink a couple, but you need to get back to your project. Four beers in, you decide to connect with your brother after you finish the remaining two beers, instant distraction. I guess you will complete your project next week; the only reason I laugh is that I lived it. Does this scenario sound familiar to you?

Laser-focused: Being laser-focused is to have complete and accurate focus when you are performing your assembly work. Being a pro assembler and knowing my job better than anyone, my attention to detail elevates. The accuracy of my operation flow is flawless. The assembly technique is extraordinary, and the execution is carried out with zero distractions. There are times in life when you need to be laser-focused; preparing for an interview, deciding to change your career, even going back to school requires you to be at the top of your game. A positive mindset makes you aware of the importance of being laser-focused, putting your best self forward, knowing your worth when pursuing a career change, and making a commitment when deciding to go back to further your education.

Total Focus: Total focus is when you give your full attention to the assembly operation; no external or internal obstacles can maneuver their way into your positive mindset. External barriers include everything you do not have any control over or say in, for example, Covid-19, your physical stature, and what other people in your work environment do.

Covid-19 changed the world as we know it. Social distancing, the wearing of masks, the inability to congregate around a large group of your friends and family. The impact has devastated weddings, picnics, businesses, and most importantly, our educational system.

Your physical stature can impact you immensely, especially in an assembly work environment. Everyone is different; we learn to make the adjustments and adaptations required to complete the task at hand.

Ergonomically, it is paramount that your position allows you to work safely, comfortably, and without any hindrance. Some people may need a stool or step ladder to complete their job, while others may need a specialized tool because they are left-handed or their gun is too heavy. We all have to adjust and adapt to new things in life. Who would have ever thought that we would be wearing masks everywhere we go or not being able to attend a concert or sporting event? That is the way of the world right now. We face a different way of living, and how we interact with one another through all this madness is a portal for positivity to come through.

Working with other people, being human is hard enough handling your own life, let alone knowing what the people around you are going to do. Some things you have no control of are people who miss work, people putting forth little or no effort on their job, and people who seem to wake up in a lousy mood every day, bringing negativity into the workplace.

The beauty of being human, however, is that even though you have no control over these external obstacles, you have the power of your positive mindset and can equally disperse positivity to those around you by your actions and attitude.

Live your life to the fullest, and regardless of the newly implemented safeguards we have due to Covid-19, we are still blessed each day we rise with the ability to be here another day. We all can succeed in this world; you can transform even those who appear to be negative into acquiring a positive mindset with the proper motivation, and feeling of self-worth and value. Positivity can overcome external obstacles.

Internal obstacles can range from process issues and supplier issues and include your mindset: fear, confusion, anger, depression, or self-doubt. These issues and emotions can prevent an individual from fulfilling goals and aspirations, and impact their work performance. We will look at these internal obstacles more deeply. Remind yourself that these apply to your daily life situation and any job or career.

As an example of a few internal obstacles, we all are aware that the list is an endless one, so take heed and apply it to your personal life situation. In our company, process and supplier issues are the responsibility of the operations team. Supervisors, engineers, material coordinators and many others provide support for the team. Their goal is to give the pro assemblers a work environment that enables them to complete the job effectively, providing both the tools and technology for the job to be successful, on time, or under cycle time.

Assembly is a process, as life is a process, and there are times when there are flaws in both. Emotions are real, positive people, and when you get your first taste of assembly work, you will experience a gamut of emotions. Asking yourself if you can do the job (doubt/fear), will you be able to retain the training you received (confusion), and the feelings you get when you are the last light on numerous cycles (anger). We control what we can, and correct those internal obstacles.

A positive mindset will get you through your training more easily; repetition and consistency are the guiding tools to your success in becoming a pro assembler. Doing away with all negative emotions as you become acclimated to your new assembly assignment will pave the way to a positive outcome and make you feel valued; we all have something to contribute. A positive mindset brings out the potential that we all have inside of us and shows the innate value that we all possess.

My positive mindset on Focus:

The vital thing to keep in mind is that the small details enable you to succeed in the task or venture that you are applying your due diligence to.

SEQUENCING

In assembly work, the sequence in which you run the operation of your job is crucial. The most important reason is that part of your process may impact another teammate on the assembly line after your station. If you forget something during that cycle, you create an obstacle for a teammate. An example, part of my job was to remove two bolts because the teammate a couple of stations up from me would be making an attachment where I had removed the bolts. On several occasions, I forgot to remove the bolts, with the result being that I added five minutes to my teammate's cycle time; this was unacceptable. Being a combination of a lack of focus, mind not being on task, and forgetfulness, it was both a hindrance and time killer to the teammate that had to call me down to remove the bolts. During my walk of shame, cursing myself, and apologizing repeatedly to my teammate, I told myself that there had to be a way for me never to miss that part of the process, mistake-proofing the issue, and creating a corrective action with a positive mindset in place.

The solution, positive people, was to change my sequence. We only build two types of machines, Machine A and Machine B; the majority of what we produce is Machine A. which required me to remove the two bolts. Machine B did not require the removal of any bolts. Whenever I saw that we were building Machine A, the first thing I would do in my new sequence would be to remove the two bolts. This prevented missing or forgetting the bolts' removal, as I made the task first in my operation cycle. It is incredible how easy it is to find a simple fix when you take a moment to look more closely at an issue or problem.

Sequencing creates consistency, based on your job's repetitive nature and the frequency of the number of machines you build. Sequencing varies; as a pro assembler, you are continuously improving your skill set. You often discover a better operation method or a situation that occurs, which brings to light why you need to change your sequence; either way, the process is made favorable by eliminating an internal obstacle and helping a teammate succeed with their respective job.

Anyone can apply sequencing to daily life situations; the order you approach and use in your everyday routine can both save you time and open up a world of opportunities and positive outcomes. Take the time to give thorough consideration to the order of your daily routine, is there anything you can do to change the sequence and make a task, goal, or dream more attainable or possibly bring your aspirations to fruition?

Sequencing can range from the way you drive to and from work, adding or removing something from your operation when an operation does not work correctly. Changing the order of how you do things often promotes a better outcome and a completed accomplishment.

My positive mindset on sequencing:

Sequencing equals consistency and organization, which reduces or eliminates errors when performing a repetitive action. No one knows you better than yourself, so a custom fit sequencing to meet your personal needs is the requirement to meet your goals.

4

COMPETITION/CHALLENGES

ositive people, competition is good for the soul, and in an assembly work environment, competition is a breeding ground of positivity and success building. I put these two together, but I want to approach them separately, thus making eight elements.

The daily approach that sets my positive mindset is as follows; twenty-one machines to build are the equivalent of a twenty-one round championship fight; each cycle to me is considered a round. My preparation and competitiveness makes me want to win every round or cycle in the assembly environment. Everyone has their routine to get ready for the day ahead, and the method people use varies from person to person or team to team.

I'm aware that I will not be the first to complete the cycle, but the positive mindset that flows through me is that of a modern-day gladiator who sets out to conquer my competition on every cycle. Competition creates two things, positive competition with some of your team members and a positive work environment as you challenge the group to be at their best, proving that we are the best pro assemblers in the entire manufacturing industry.

Most people go to work to do their jobs and go home at the end of the shift; competitive team members strive to get their cycle done as expeditiously as possible. Some set up for the next cycle, while others are on their cell phones, as most of them are, just keeping it real here, positive people.

Those of us who are competitive will, on occasion, remind that competitive team member that works next to our station that we are going to knock them out on the next cycle. Competition makes team members more determined to perform at a higher level, but at a faster pace so they will finish before you. That makes for productive competition and outstanding performances on an individual basis.

The same goes for when you challenge yourself or your teammates. People can exceed any obstacle when they put their minds to it. The group of pro assemblers that I work with often show and prove that capability daily, completing a cycle time in eighteen, nineteen , or twenty minutes, nineteen or twenty times in a shift.

The team displays a high-level performance collectively, and it shows the ability to exceed any challenge we may have to face throughout the shift.

Individual challenges may be to beat the fastest

cycle time that you ever ran, enhance your performance by making sure you double-check your work to avoid any missed operation. Help a teammate out when you can help them save time during their cycle; that is teamwork at the highest level.

When people work for a common goal and the incentive is making more money, the results can be phenomenal.

Positive people challenge themselves daily, regardless of the task or job that they are doing. We can all better ourselves with a positive mindset; I am a living witness to seeing new assemblers transform into pro assemblers. Initially, frustration had set in with the newness of the job. Still, by encouraging them and providing positive affirmation, they developed the confidence needed to reach a level of mastering their craft and adding value to the team.

Please take a moment to listen to what I am saying; the word "Challenge" alone brings with it a sense of accountability and responsibility. A person or team is brought to a duel, to face an obstacle or adversary; in assembly, the obstacle may be missing parts, missing people, equipment failure. The adversaries are time and your teammates; you are hoping that time does not run out on you, and the teammates you work with are worthy and equally talented opponents. The goal is to get it done first!

My positive mindset on competition/challenges:

Win, win, win!!! Strive to be a fierce competitor, always looking to be the best at whatever it is you do. Challenging yourself to improve and continuously grow sustains a positive mindset because you can share your knowledge with others and pay it forward.

5

QUALITY-DRIVEN

Quality-Driven is an attainable attribute that anyone can develop. It is as simple as if you were custom making your own home or the car of your dreams. The person who is paying over half a million dollars for the machine you are building for them deserves to have their investment made with nothing less than the highest quality. Being able to leave the assembly line after your shift, knowing that you gave your best effort to ensure that you did your part to make that customer trust and believe in the machine they will be using to get the job done, is priceless.

A positive mindset sets in motion the purpose of what actions you perform daily; quality-driven practices make you pay attention to all aspects of your assembly efforts. Taking pride in your work performance and achieving new milestones. Take a moment to think about the things you buy for yourself, family members, or even friends. What is it that you demand? Quality, and if you do not receive the quality you desire, you're not going to buy it, or you will spread the word that the quality was not up to par and not give a positive recommendation.

Feedback, praise, accolades that we receive as a team from our customers is the driving force that makes you want to produce a machine built with the highest quality.

Being quality-driven is an essential element and fits your daily lifestyle and can be applied to any job or career. In the assembly world, quality is an everyday topic. Quality issues missed by a pro assembler may occur; the team has often contributed to catching and correcting any possible error that got through. That is the real importance of teamwork. Pro assemblers see the same process day after day, so when an operation does not look right, reported information for corrective action helps everyone.

I represent the quality segment in my assembly area; the job entails informing the team where we stand on achieving our quality goals, which we have met throughout the year. The feeling is incredible; the entire assembly team works as a collective unit, giving their best effort with quality being one of the crucial parts of building a great machine.

Integrity in quality is as vital as performing the process at the highest level because as a pro assembler or whatever job or career you have, doing it right the first time saves both time and money. On the assembly line, we have a code of ethics; some of those codes are never to let an operation or mistake move forward without fixing it or informing someone that there is an issue. See something; say something. Be ethical, do the right thing by the customer you're building that respective machine for, build the machine like you were making it for yourself. Lastly, press innovation, there are always opportunities to refine and enhance your skill set. Stay steadfast to being quality-driven, and you will be able to put yourself among the elite in your job, career, or daily lifestyle.

My positive mindset on quality-driven:

Being quality-driven is a never-ending quest to be the best, striving to accomplish any given task that you are asked to complete or perform to the best of your ability.

6

THE IMPORTANCE OF EFFICIENCY

Efficiency is merely the catalyst for self-improvement. I find myself on an endless quest to become more efficient. The incentive is always to work smarter, not harder; being efficient allows for opportunities for innovation, skill set improvement, and sharing knowledge with your teammates for their advancement in self-improvement. To me, efficiency is a relationship of giving and taking, which is of mutual benefit for all involved.

The beginning of the build season was a taxing experience. I spent most of my time walking back and forth to get the parts I needed to get through the allotted time cycle. My efficiency level was substandard at best; my cycle time was nineteen minutes out of the twenty-one minutes; this meant I was busting my butt from start to finish. This lack of efficiency meant that I had little to no time to even prepare for the next machine, and that is a lot of wear and tear on your body, yet it is self-inflicted.

The changing point for me was when a teammate came down to help me out one day. It is surprising what you can learn from a different set of eyes surveying and observing your work area and how you work your cycle. He asked me why my parts were so far away and suggested that I condense my work area footprint. Taking heed of his advice, I was able to cut five minutes off of my cycle time. It was the beginning of an obsession with becoming as efficient as possible and sharing that knowledge with the team, so that everyone had the option to improve their work area.

Teammates know me for having a few sayings; one of my favorite sayings is, "Come on, y'all"! That is my go-to motivational catchphrase because it is always said before we start the workday. I am providing a positive affirmation to the team, which jump-starts everyone in having a productive day. I make a note to tell my teammates that they are the best pro assemblers in the entire industry and I know they believe me when I tell them.

Another phrase that I regularly tell the team is "set yourself up for success" because no one else will. Whenever I say to the team that it is time to go into "beast mode," they all know that we need to kick it into high gear covering all aspects; productivity, quality, and safety.

My positive mindset on efficiency:

We can all continuously improve ourselves, continually seeking ways to enhance our life's processes and work performance; being self-innovative and creative brings efficiency to fruition. Being efficient in your skill set adds value, making you an asset in all situations.

7

TIME MANAGEMENT

In the assembly world, time management is everything because once you get behind, you begin to feel as if time is going at warp speed, which makes it difficult for you to get caught back up. Positive people, we are all aware that time is the one thing that you can never get back, and when you utilize your time correctly, you gain the ability to do great things in your life.

When you think about it, life goes by in the blink of an eye. When you are young, you feel invincible, and you believe that you have all the time in the world. In your teen years, you have that mindset of "I will be glad when I am grown, and then I will do whatever I want". Twenty-one rolls around, and you are officially a grownup. You may be in school, or you may be working, both admirable, but time stops for no one.

Suddenly you hit twenty-five, and all of a sudden, it

is thirty, thirty-five, forty, forty-five, fifty, and currently fifty-five. The point here, positive people; is as I stated earlier, your life's two critical dates are your birth date and your death date. It is how you utilize your time and manage your time between these two essential dates that build a foundation for your legacy as a person; this management separates you from others and keeps you on a timeline for success.

When I decided to go back to school to earn my degree, it took me a couple of years to make my mind up, asking myself, "Is this really what you want to do?" I worked full-time at various hours, eight to twelve hours a day, six days a week mostly. Time and money were the determining factors in my decision. I will share this point with you, positive people; there is no bigger dream killer than procrastination, which equates to letting time slip away that you will never get back.

Once I made my mind up to continue with my education, time management became a requirement. I had to perform my job at a high level for the entire shift; then, I had to go home, do homework, or attend a seminar twice a week. There was no room for wasting any time and believe me, there were days when I second-guessed myself, but by staying positive, time became my most excellent ally. Allow it to be yours as well.

My positive mindset on time management:

When you manage your time right, you can seize the moment in real-time. Knowing that time lost is time gone forever, do not lose the opportunity to develop yourself, and stay on your grind. Procrastination is waiting for you to get to it tomorrow, will tomorrow ever come? Come on, y'all!

8

SET YOURSELF UP FOR SUCCESS

I f there is one thing that I have learned in fifty-five years of living, positive people, it is that you have to "Set yourself up for success." Ask any teammate in my respective area, and they will tell you that they have heard that message from me on multiple occasions. Ask me why, and I will reply because it holds true to the growth and development of yourself as a person and an above-average worker, in our case, pro assemblers.

Each morning when I arrive at work, I am aware that we will be building twenty-one machines. The process entails putting on equally twenty-one air filters, brackets, and on specific machines, a valve that I must prepare in advance.

My positive mindset tells me that for me to have a successful cycle and a productive day, the regime of being proactive in my job ensures that I win that cycle, completing my operation faster than the set time allotted.

Preparation manifests positive success in people, and no one can set you up to win better than yourself.

The twist that goes with setting yourself up for success is that under different circumstances, you can also assist someone else to be successful. Whether you are assembling, working another career, or helping someone in your life, the boost of confidence and encouragement is enormous.

When I decided to continue my education and pursue a degree at fifty-one years of age, the decision was not easy. There was soul-searching, commitment, time, and motivation that needed consideration in every aspect of my aspiration. The need to be set up for success came to the forefront immediately; that is when I came up with my concept of becoming "selfish," not selfish in the standard term but my approach to the journey I was about to experience.

My personal view of being selfish and please hear me on this, positive people, is being self-motivated, having self-determination and initiative, being selfless, and, most importantly, self-starting. The mindset that you convey provides the drive and confidence required to meet any goal and aspiration that you want to achieve. Still, when you are "selfish," it enables you to combine the elements mentioned above into fruition and accomplishments.

My positive mindset on setting yourself up for success:

Positive people, we all have one life to live; opportunities for greatness are achievable when you apply your inner strength and push yourself past the barriers that try to hold you down. Do not be the person scared to ask for help, because it is all up to you in the end. Success is limitless when you take the time to put in the work, and make a choice.

EPILOGUE

When it comes to being positive, it is a natural thing for me, never forced nor faked, truly second nature in the current times that I am living. The greatest reward for me is to be able to share my positivity with everyone around me. Please allow me to clarify myself, positive people, when I say "everyone," I speak of every human being around me. People are people; diversity and differences make up the opportunities to learn and grow from one another. Of course, we do not live in a perfect world, and there are times that life brings us challenges that seem impossible. I promise you this, with a positive mindset, achievements and accomplishments flourish daily.

Being positive does not cost you a dime, and you are not required or forced to be. You are free from any pressure because you and you alone have the choice to decide how to treat others in a respectful and good-natured attitude. The return you will receive is a mutual feeling of gratitude and kindness from other positive people who cross your path.

When I share my positive mindset and motivation with others, I never expect to get praise or recognition in return. The reward that I get from having a positive attitude and sharing that with others is when I can see a change in an individual. A person may have been struggling with their job, turning them positive helps them become better, and now they have the confidence that was always inside the person. Seeing the change in negative people's attitudes is exhilarating and a much-needed transformation in the assembly work environment.

We all know the saying, "It's not what you know; it's who you know." I have learned that this statement is accurate. When you have a reputation for being positive and motivating, people take notice of that positivity and listen to what you have to say, knowing that you are speaking from the heart for the good of those around you.

Being a pro assembler and being surrounded by other pro assemblers makes me happy to be part of an elite group of individuals who can consistently come to work daily and face challenges together as a formidable team. My greatest strength is helping others and bringing people together. To me, there is nothing better then sharing what you know with someone else to make them better or taking a diverse group of people and convincing them to be great, above-average, and winners.

My positive mindset teaches me that there is no limit

to the opportunities that life has to offer, and the only thing that can stop you is yourself. At fifty-five and being in the next chapter of my existence, my number one goal is to develop myself into the most positive person I can be, and share that positivity with others. Thank you for joining me on this journey; stay blessed.

ACKNOWLEDGMENTS

This first book is a personal achievement that has been running through my mind for the past two years while I worked the assembly line, day in and day out. My first acknowledgment is, "Thanks be to God," for blessing me with the ability to set, research, work steadily, and to complete my personal goals.

I want to show my appreciation and love to all the people who loved, supported, and inspired me throughout writing my first book. It means the world to me knowing that people believe in me and are waiting for the release of Assembly Required: A Guide to Building a Positive Mindset.

To my mother, Sandra Bullock (And no, not the actress!!!), and my father, Ernest Benson (R.I.H.), I love you both very much. My mother is my inspiration; our birthdays are three days apart, and it was my mother who gave me the gift of seeing the good in people and helping anyone that may be in need. My mother has always supported and positively reinforced that a strong work ethic and persistence will always pay off.

I got my smile from my father, and I will tell you this, I am so thankful to have that quality feature. He left this world way too early, but I know he is looking down on me with his beautiful smile and side-busting laugh of his and saying, "Do your thing, son, do your thing!"

My sister and brother (My mothers' side), Nilea and Vernell, are the best big sister and brother a person could ever have. They have always supported and instilled in me to be a leader. My sister is one of the strongest women I know and taught me to speak my mind because that is my given right. My brother is one of the smartest people that I have ever known. He is and will forever be my role model. I love you both.

My sisters and brother (My father's side), Sawanda, Angel, Bonnie, and Ernest, I am the oldest of five siblings on my father's side. I love you all equally, and although we did not grow up together, we have developed a bond instilled in us by our father. Let us always keep in touch.

To my kids, Tyshianique, Terell, and Tyrae Jr., I love you all more than anything; you're grown and on your own, but you know how we Townzel's are; the bond and love between us is an unbreakable one, and I know you are all destined for greatness. Much love to all my grandkids as well!!!

To the influencing factors behind this book, I want to thank all of my union sisters and brothers, THE PRO ASSEMBLERS, and everyone else who contributes to the goal that we strive for every season. Building the best damn machines made, by the best people, hands down, worldwide!

To all of my Purdue University Global classmates, we all set out to achieve our educational goals and vowed to change the world. That opportunity is now; I wish you all blessings and prosperity in your journey and sustain that achievement momentum.

Special thanks to Dr. Jason Jackson; you were more than just my professor and mentor. The guidance that you shared with me whenever I became overwhelmed was a real blessing. There was no sugar coating or appeasement; you forever kept it honest and reminded me that everything worthwhile entailed hard work and dedication of self. Respect and love for you, the knowledge you gave me changed my life.

To the most important people, THANK YOU, my readers. You are the reason that I write and share what is on my mind. Without you, I am nothing; maybe we can change the world for the better; one reader at a time, and by sharing and spreading your positivity with others. Find the greatness inside of yourself. I know it is there; you need to seek it, then build upon it. Stay blessed; Come on, y'all!

ABOUT THE AUTHOR

Tyrae Townzel Sr. was born in Iowa City, IA, on February 13, 1965. He has worked in the manufacturing industry for twenty plus years and recently earned his Bachelor's Degree in Business Administration with a concentration in Supply Chain Management and Logistics from Purdue University Global with honors, at fifty-four. He inspires others to help them find their better self, and creates positivity within all people of the world, working together to achieve that goal.

Made in the USA
Monee, IL
28 February 2021

61549043R00032